I0165980

H. Philips Montgomery

Tadmor, the Pride of the Desert

H. Philips Montgomery

Tadmor, the Pride of the Desert

ISBN/EAN: 9783743317253

Manufactured in Europe, USA, Canada, Australia, Japa

Cover: Foto ©ninafisch / pixelio.de

Manufactured and distributed by brebook publishing software
(www.brebook.com)

H. Philips Montgomery

Tadmor, the Pride of the Desert

The Pride of the Desert.

BY

H. PHILIPS MONTGOMERY.

BOSTON:
ROBERTS BROTHERS.
PHILADELPHIA: CHARLES DESILVER.
1865.

Entered according to Act of Congress, in the year 1864, by

H. PHILIPS MONTGOMERY,

in the Clerk's Office of the District Court of the United States for the Eastern
District of Pennsylvania.

.

UNIVERSITY PRESS:
WELCH, BIGELOW, AND COMPANY,
CAMBRIDGE.

CANTO I.

THE COUNCIL.

CANTO I.

THE COUNCIL.

DEEP in the Orient, now, alas ! entombed,
 Surrounded by a vast and trackless moor,
Which drank her beryl waters, Tadmor bloomed.
Her fearless sons did whilom conquering pour
From arrowy Tigris to the Nilus' shore ;
But scarce the Sea had waved her triumph-tongue,
Her hautboy's blast and bursting peal of war
Italia heard ! Rome's temple-gates were swung ;
Palmyra quivered not ! and how she fell, my song.

I.

The thirsting sands of Syrian plain
Bid sad adieu to night again.
And now aloft the day has won
Each cedar-top of Lebanon.
The encircled caravan unwinds
 Once more its drowsy coil ;
The drooping camel gladly finds
 Fair Suri's softening soil.

For since the Iran waters told
Their wavelet parting, naught had lulled
Their slumber save the desert's breath,
And Simoom's seething blast of death.

II.

Oh, 't is a beauteous sight to see
The morn's first blush on Stromboli!
But gorgeous where with earliest light
Palmyra bursts upon the sight!
A thousand glittering towers beam;
A thousand sparkling minarets gleam;
From column, dome, and colonnade, —
On these the skilful Scopas made
His name immortal, — shaft and base,
And capital of Corinth's grace,
Reflection springs; as when on high
The Polar spirits light their sky,
And spread auroral archway o'er
The northern zone from shore to shore.

III.

Aloft, e'en temple-dome above,
Are terraced aisle and cooling grove.
The wearied eye glad lingers now
Where tendril, rose, and leafy bough,
Be-drooped with dew, their precious breath

Send showering to the plain beneath
From amaranth and Suri flowers
So sweetly, that fair Eden's bowers
In all their bloom were scarce more fair;
And th' Almighty trained the blossom there!

IV.

Afar, Euphrates' wave is seen
To sprinkle wide her matin-sheen.
Proud flood! what empires hast thou known
Since Chaos fell, and Earth was born?
Thy gladsome waters swept the vales
Of Paradise, while choral gales
Hymned sweetly in quaternion flow,
And echoing came and soft and low
From each thy sacred sister-flood,
And praised Him, Maker of all good!

V.

Temptation was not absent long,
Fair Ede, and cursed with withering Wrong
Thy beauteous bloom. Thy wandering wave
Then knew not Earth, nor where to lave.

VI.

Then reigned Chaldea's "King of Kings"
Where Tigris to Euphrates brings

Her fleetest foam : and Man forswore
The Great Omnipotent !   His doom
Enkindled, spread a blackening gloom
Upon the earth ; from Heaven's shore
And th' empyrean's copious deeps
Upbroken did the waters pour !
Till Ararat's most lofty steeps
Sank down into the gurgling main !
The ocean-wave was monarch then.

VII.

But soon thy currents poured anew,
Euphrates, but in darker hue ;
And traced their deep and erring line
To Babylonia's impious shrine.
Her tower crumbled, while each tongue,
Though uttering, was unknown :
Dissentient voices came among
Mankind, and Man was lone !

VIII.

Then next th' Assyrian dipped his steel
In thy fair stream, and stamped the heel
Of power on thy groaning shore
For ages ! and great Babylon rose.
Her sparkling splendor soon was o'er ;
For Heaven told her dismal woes !

And 'mid her deep damnation's throes,
The Persian and the roving Mede
Unstrung his bow, unreined his steed
Upon yon sands. Then from the West
The mighty Macedonian came ;
For humbled Europe had confessed —
Though Hellas loathe — his boundless fame.
He oped the Cilician portals wide,
Where Taurian mount meets Taurus' side,
And heeding not the Asian foe,
He joyed in Iran's orient glow.

IX.

The conqueror sighed his sword uphung,
The clarion soon his requiem rung !
Then Roma sang her battle-pæan,
Unfurled her bright imperial sheen
From Madaï to Senaär.
The Chaldean marks a stranger star, —
The Kasdim in their brazen towers
Knew all the orbs, and knew their hours, —
The star on Juda rests ! Again,
Thou storied river ! thy glad wave
Re-echoed the night-wind's whispering strain ;
And with thy flowing murmur gave
All-joyous homage to the Throne
Of Him Triune, and yet but One.

His brow ungemmed, no court was there,
No bright monarchal spangling shone,
No train of pomp, no gilded glare :
He reigned unbugled, bannerless,
With but th' Adoring Mother's kiss,
And angel's voice to crown Him King !
Thou wouldst to His Dominion cling !
But Roma hushed thy wavelet-songs.
Once more to Syria now belongs
The fair Euphrates ; and her own
Is claimed by Tadmor for her throne.
But cease ; the pages yet to come
Will tell her glory, mourn her doom !

X.

Behold ! the day his blushing bride
The roseate morn leads down the side
Of Lebanon, while fount and fell,
And leaf and shrub in Suri's dell,
Joins in the bridal chorus loud
Of merriest nature, while the cloud
With morn-tints spangled throws her sheen,
An azured veil, upon the scene.

XI.

Now brightly burns the vestal fire ;
Now sweetly chants the temple-choir ;

Tow'rets and minarets sparkle higher
  To greet the glorious Sun !
The censers fast their cassia fling ;
The choristry more joyous sing ;
While clanging chimes harmonious ring
  Thence cadence into one.
For scarce has echo hushed her flow,
The jocund morn is draped in woe.

XII.

Why ceased the choral morning song ?
Why stilled the chancel's votive tongue ?
Why from the palace and the cot —
These equal love their own begot —
Wild sorrowing comes ? the mother's moan
Like that in Judah's Ramah known
When Rachel childless wept her own ?

XIII.

From Taurus' hills through Syria's aisles
A Syrian host in confused files
To Tadmor streams ! their banners torn,
Their serried ranks impetuous borne
By Rome's wild cohorts, as the leaves
Are shattered by th' autumnal blast,
Where flowery Sibma vainly grieves
Her summer-sheen is sweeping past !

XIV.

Full soon the offspring of great Jove
And Themis, circling, sadly move
To noon and eve.   Now list the calls
From shrilly clarions wide resound,
And winding turn in swift rebound, —
As when the storm on Etna falls,
And thrills her fiery-caverned ground.

XV.

To th' accited Council chief and sage
Troop in the measured step of age ;
Statesman, and soldier whose proud form
Ne'er quivered in the battle storm !
The Council met.   A seething sound
Like that of waves which fell around
Baal-Zephon's shoal, when Orion urged
The Red-Sea waves so that they surged
Beneath her sands ; till morning watch
Sweet Miriam sang in joyous glee,
" The Chosen walk a pathwayed sea !
This morn in vain the watery search
For Pharaoh and his chariotry ! "

XVI.

Hushed now the voice and eager tongue,
  And warriors' clashing steel
Which on the marbled pave had rung,
  And swells the hautboy peal ;
And burst the trumpets to the dome !
While sways the throng like Norway's trees
When howls the Arctic's wildest breeze.
'T is he, the great Longinus, come !
He casts one glance of pride around
The numerous host ; one well may see
His nature noble and as free,
By guile nor arcane malice bound.
Th' Almighty's ban but lightly traced
Its withering line on one so graced.
No self is there : by millions deemed
A Great Palladium, he but seemed
At Suri's shrine devout to stand, —
That shrine his Country, his own Land.

XVII.

The bugle-strain is still more shrill,
The trumpet-blast is louder still,
As, beauteous, yet in martial mien,
Appears the gorgeous " Orient Queen."

Her form is woman's utmost grace ;
A mind reflects in that fair face
And brilliant eye, the spirits stern
Such as in women rarely burn, —
Spirits which on the battle-field
Could charge the foe, nor ask the shield !
Dark Pride has marked her brow with care,
For Beauty loves to revel there.
So proud and fair, yon Queen may claim
The blood of Egypt's fairest fame,
And Macedonia's nobler name.

XVIII.

High on a throne, — all fretted wrought
In gems from Ind and Ophir brought,
Where Oman's dark and surgy Sea
Gives precious pearls to Araby, —
Zenobia viewed the countless throng.
She waved each harp and lute and song
Which heralded her coming, cease !
Then, soft as rainbow's gentle kiss
On great Niagara's feathery foam,
Or as from Sinai's deep abyss
The morning calls the woody gloom,
While anxious echo left her cell
In dome and arch, her accents fell : —

XIX.

"My Palmyrenians, ye well know,
By sad Orontes' waters' flow
At Emesa and Antioch
Resounded far the battle shock!
When Suri with Italia clashed,
In vain our hissing fire flashed;
In vain my furious horsemen clove
Their foe's strong rank, and filled the grove
With Roman blood; in vain their steel;
The maddened foe in frenzied reel
But gathered strength, — as waves which sweep
The rapids, ere they plunge the steep,
When some rock-isle impedes their flow.
One moment heard Rome's battle-pæan;
One moment glowed her standards' sheen.
Now, Syria, list thy peal of woe!
The bugles' sound, the ordered tread,
Like spirit-marching of the dead,
Now nearer comes; each bellowing hill
Back hurls their shout, while clarions thrill
The wide terrene! A moment more
Palmyra's victory was o'er!
The Roman's triumph-chant was sung;
The Syrian's dirge was faintly rung;
For many a dying hero there

Had but the requiem of the air :
His winding-sheet his armor cold,
   The mountain rock his bier ;
His cold clay heeds not costly fold
   Whose spirit knew not fear.

XX.

"Aurelian, with furious speed,
To Tadmor comes ; he doth not heed
The foe, nor famine, nor the blast
Which sounds her death-knell wild and fast.
When he from Taurus mount shall burst,
And in our stream shall slake his thirst,
Our pleasant plants then no more green ;
Our merry vineyard-shouting ceased,
When evening in amethyst
Bids rest from toil ; no more then seen
The tendril clinging to the bough,
Nor heard our gushing streamlets' flow !

XXI.

"Say, then, ye sons of lone Tadmor,
Ye who fear not the rage and roar
Of battle's tempest, shall this flood
Be poured on Suri ? or your blood
Be driven through your fevered vein
By heaving heart, that once again,

With earnest hate and eager zeal,
In Rome's proud ranks ye dash your steel ?

XXII.

" Say first, Longinus, thou great sage ;
Thou who art learned in wisdom's page ;
Hast plucked from Hellas' richest vines,
Hast delved into her deepest mines,
And brought that richest mineral forth,
Of daring courage, untold worth !
Land of Leonidas, and thee,
Self-doomèd Solon, thou wouldst be
Alone with these, of glorious fame,
Though in a desert without name ! "

XXIII.

Zenobia ceased.   Longinus stood ;
In majesty of thought he viewed
The anxious host ; with deep despair
He wrestled, not debasing fear,
Strained now each eye, and turned each ear : —

XXIV.

" Queen of the Orient, and ye peers,
I too have seen the wounds and tears
Of Syrian soldier, and his home,
The clash of hosts, the battle's foam.

'T is true th' Abana's waters flow
To Pharphar's wave and sands below,
Ensanguined with Palmyra's slain;
Though ours the loss, yet theirs the gain.

XXV.

"Whose blood to his own land is given
Constant breathes to highest Heaven!
More honor in his cere-cloth's mould
Than Colchian colors, Hermean gold.
Fair Suri sheds her sweetest bloom
Where soldier sleeps in patriot's tomb!

XXVI.

"E'en now the Hesperian gale doth bring
The hammers' fall, the clink and ring
Of Gothic arms and clashing shields
In wild Hyrcinia's woody fields.
When winter builds a pathway o'er
The Danube's flood to Thracian shore,
Then Rome her cohorts soon may need,
Each lance and bow, each foaming steed.

XXVII.

"The Persian king has learned to know
To Tadmor better friend than foe;
While from the South, the copious Nile

Her Memphian horse and swarthy file
Shall pour upon yon Roman host.
These burning sands our ramparts strong ;
Here Rome shall build her holocaust,
With plenteous death and requiem song !
My life to Tadmor and my Queen
I give ! and, by the morn's bright sheen,
Which spangles now yon orby dome,
I but in death see conquering Rome ! "

XXVIII.

A shadow crossed his glowing brow,
As night-shade glooms the waters' flow.
Longinus paused ; convulsed with thought,
He strove to deem the shade was naught.
His patriot eye was dimmed ; his frame
Heaved once, and only once, with shame.
Again his voice, but quivering, came : —

XXIX.

" More fatal is the mining slow
Of occult mind, than open foe ;
The oak bends not with wildest wind, ╱
But by the worm we fagots bind.
At Thermos' gates, where Œtan dell
The ocean meets, the Spartan fell !
The Persian power stormed in vain ;
A *Greek* betrayed, the Greeks were slain !

XXX.

"O Palmyrenians! should I find
Betrayal in a Syrian mind,
As joyous as the Teuton's pall
When in the strife his captains fall
Would be my death! nor should ye grieve,
For living death 't would be to live!"

XXXI.

As through the magnet's unseen vein
The amber flows, or as the rain
From high Armenia's mountain-snow
Doth swell each fount and stream below,
So did Longinus' voice and mien
Flow through the throng; and each was seen
To glow with new-awakened fire.
Soldier and sage, each son and sire
Clanked his steel, or waved his hair.
'T is silence, though the echoing air
Is loath to lose Longinus' word.
Again Zenobia's voice is heard : —

XXXII.

"My sons of Suri! who is here
And deems us lost, or shrinks with fear?
When he, our bravest, — if there be

The bravest, 'mid such bravery, —
Fair Tadmor deems and life but one,
And joys in death her past renown?

XXXIII.

"Well do I know no suasion need
To urge ye to heroic deed!
Then be each arm a mighty host
In will and daring, though the cost
Be death. Yet shall a Roman die!
Our God shall tint your panoply
With colors gorgeous, and as rare —
If we may earth to Heaven compare —
As Christians say their Great on High
Doth gild His own who faithful die!
Primal of all, when Cœle-Syria's dell,
Hushed in repose, no jarring sound shall tell,
Let all Palmyra to our Temple throng,
To urge on high due praise and votive song
To Him, All-Glorious Orb, whose eterne Light
Knows not Earth's fleeting morn, nor hour, nor night!"

XXXIV.

The Assembly o'er, now heard the fall
Of ponderous iron; fosse and wall
With thousands teem; the liquid flame
Crackles and seethes: such sound there came

When Salem fell and passed away, —
Such was Jehovah's doom ; — then day
And night were one, for through the gloom,
The flash, and hiss, and bursting boom
Of chargëd fire did disthrone
The star-crowned god. Now, one by one,
The balista and tower strong
In labent groove are dragged along.
The creeking wheel heaps up the sand
In hugest mounds, for close at hand
The Roman doth his engines bring.
But list yon sacred bells' wild swing !
Their pealing chimes are loud and clear,
And call to temple and to prayer.

XXXV.

What pen can write, whose voice can tell,
Of Tadmor's temple ere she fell ?
Bewildered Fancy guides her wing
Where Contemplation may not soar ;
And yet from aeriest heights may bring
No sheen more bright than sprinkles o'er
Yon wondrous fabric, or more pure !

XXXVI.

Of massive strength, yet graceful form,
Unmoved, untinged by wildest storm

That bleaky Caucasus could blow,
When Boreas hurls his mountain snow,
Each fluted shaft and architrave,
And pure and white, the moon doth lave ;
Delighted in their carvëd cells,
Like ocean's voice in Oman's shells, —
So white and pure, the Orient star,
    Bright gnomon to the morn,
Will leave one gleam to linger there
    To greet the coming dawn !
Innumerous lights are showered wide,
    Like aerolites that gleam
O'er Bab-el-Mandeb's boisterous tide,
    Where whirls her tropic stream.

XXXVII.

Pride of the world ! thy temple-brow
Must need be strong, and deep below
Thy fountain-deeps must be thy walls !
E'en then those rocks and columned halls
Shall by the shivering wind be blown ;
Thy very site unsearched, unknown,
Till Arab, wandering o'er the plain,
Shall pile thy friezed and fretted fane,
And rudely drag, with heating toil,
Thy slumbering arches from the soil :
And through long ages yet to be,

Yon sad and sorrowing cypress-tree
Alone shall tell it bloomed with thee!

XXXVIII.

Now throng through the temple's every aisle
Palmyra's thousands, file on file
Continuous pours, and helmet clanks
With helmet, as the martial ranks,
With heads uncovered, bend the knee
 In silence and in awe!
But ne'er to foe could such things be
 When heard the shouts of war.
Now timbrels, lutes, and sacred song
 In chords consociate flow,
And sweep like whirlwind wild along,
 Enwrapping all below.
Then from aloft the sounds quick reel
From cymbals' crash and trumpets' peal.

XXXIX.

Now wave the censers in the air,
Blazes the cressets' brightest glare;
A thousand hands fast hold the strings,
Ten thousand strings vibrate no more,
As, white as snow, where Hyems flings
Her purest mantle on the floor
Of dreary Zembla, comes the train

Of priests, whose robes are sprinkled o'er
With flashing sardius and ligure.
Quick every harp is full again;
And emerald and jasper bright
Vie with the lustres' streaming light, —
For India's islets scarce may boast,
Trinacria's golden-showered coast,
Or Pactolus, or Hermes' stream,
Such gems as on yon white robes gleam.
The altars, heaped with offerings rare,
Their incensed flames throw high in air.
But list! the lutes have ceased their flow,
   And silence binds the minstrelsy!
While in deep tone and measure slow
   Is heard the chancel's solemn plea.

THE PRAYER.

I.

"Thou mightiest of orbs! sprung from that voice
Which rang in heavenly echo through the gloom
Of jarring chaos; then the furious Etnas hurled
Down tumbling to the floods their smoking tops;
The whirling oceans roared and gulfed them fast
And seething to their fiery-angered deeps;
Such desolation then, that swiftest sphere,

Malignant deemed of earth, enjoyed the scene,
As starry systems plunged through elemental war!
On th' empyrean's loftiest mountain-height
Thou stoodst! then sprang each wildly-roaming orb,
And found her azured groove. Soon countless harps
To flowing harmony were tuned, which since
And ceaseless have their hymning chorals wound
In winding morning-song their praise to Thee!"

CHORISTRY.

Almighty Orb! Most High of Power!
Hear our Prayer, and mark the Plea!
Soon comes Palmyra's trial-hour,
Be Thou with us, "Ηλιε!

II.

"Or if by blasting heat, or moist exhale
Of dampening dew and pestilential chill,
Or darkness deep, as when th' Egyptian groped,
And cursed the land of Goshen, which had caused
Such grief upon the Nile, to Thee best known;
So that yon proud and daring Roman host,
Which, impious, would assail thy chosen shrine,
May be from Asia to Europa hurled!
Thence evermore our flames shall constant burn,
Our glad and grateful hymns shall follow Thee
From glowy Persia to the Great-Sea deep,

Where Hesperus with fading beam now calls
The Sea-rose from its amber-shrouded couch
To greet rejoicing Thee, all-glorious Sun!

CHORISTRY.

Almighty Orb! Most High of Power!
Hear our Prayer, and mark the Plea!
Soon comes Palmyra's trial-hour,
Be thou with us, *"Ηλιε* !

CANTO II.

THE SIEGE.

CANTO II.

THE SIEGE.

NOW empire with an empire strives for sway;
  Thadmora hurls defiance to great Rome;
Through Cœle-Syria's purple-flowered way
  The blasting tramps of angry cohorts come.
Her once cerulean skies are dimmed in gloom,
  While portents dark of ill on Suri throng.
Zion betrayed *her* trust, — she found her doom!
  Defiant was her pride, and sweet her song,
Yet Salem's willowed harps in Shinar were unstrung!

I.

The clarion rings on mountain steep,
The Roman host upsprings from sleep;
And loud and shrill the tuba strain
Calls to the cohorts, "March again!"

II.

Twelve times the hour-glass had told
Its dreamy tale; as oft had rolled

From winded horn the " night-watch change."
The tents are struck ; in 'customed range
The beasts of burden wait the blast
To bear their toil. It comes full fast !
The camp is silence, for their tread
Already sounds from woody glade.

III.

In discord dull, the plumbean tramp,
The heavy-armor's clink and clamp,
The lituus peal, and chargers' stamp
On the echoing rock, comes not so shrill
As voices from yon startled hill !
For many years of beauteous peace
Had smiled on Sibma's flowery leas.

IV.

A Roman soldier, loath to leave
Orontes' blooming flowered shore,
Strayed gladly where the Great-Sea tide
Its blue wave heaves on Syria's side,
And mused the Past, its glories o'er !

V.

" Thou Monarch Sea, thy waves still roll,
While earth's proud thrones have bid thee oft
To mark their deeds ! and now the lull

Of thy night-spray is heard aloft,
Nor brings their echo to its toll !
They called the isles in all thy deep !
And slumber now in wakeless sleep.

VI.

" Where now their triremes, and the hosts
  Of shields which glimmered on thy coasts ?
  Silent and low, in the dark ocean-dell,
  Where the coralline, building his snowy-white cell,
  Has more voice than they, though in full-swelling
      pride
  They skimmed the warm tropic to India's tide.

VII.

" Where now the rainbow-tinted blaze
  Of pageantry, which stunned the gaze
  Of Cydnus' banks, when Nile's dark queen
  In flowing palace glided by ?
  Where now e'en Rome's imperial sheen
  Of Actium, and her Argosy ?

VIII.

" There Tyre, on her sapphire throne,
  In spangled splendor whilom shone !
  By sea-floods crowned, a gorgeous queen,
  Enrobed in azure and in green,

3

Her sceptre dripping with the spray
Of far-off isles, held monarch sway!

IX.

"No more the groaning timber glides
From Lebanon's exhaustless sides!
No more the moist and weeded keel
Is dragged up on the lab'ring wheel,
Till Hyem's feathery winds are o'er
No more the Tyrian marks the star
The royal-born Harpalyce;
And furls his sail, or holds the oar,
As her light shimmers on the sea!

X.

"O many a hand on the emerald floor
Of the Persian waters, has groped for Tadmor!
And, Tarshish, thy mariner, joyous and free,
As he furled his swan-wing in the foam of this sea,
And he thought of his pearl, and, fair Tadmor, of
    thee!

XI.

"Thy wave resilient shuns those walls
Where Tyre held her festivals!
Alas! now there the glazèd owl,
The bittern's cry, and famish-howl

Of roving wolf, where once the dove
Told soft her matin-tale of love.
And Zor and beauteous Saida seem
Lone desolation, and a dream !

XII.

" Nations have but an humble span
Of time their own, — and so with man !
His life a mount : the joyous child
Quick-bounding climbs ; through wooded wild
And myrtled grove he loves to stray,
And pluck the primrose by the way.
He sports with shadows, mocks dull care,
And seeks the sun-light's vertic glare.
No storm is there, no howling blast ;
The future all, and none the past.

XIII.

" Midsummer dons her deepest green ;
The child, now man, sees what hath been.
With eager step, aloft he seeks —
Ambition led — the highest peaks.
Man drinks but of a Circean bowl,
Who gains alone the *human* goal.
Th' Acropolis won, his crownëd wreath
    Its verdure but an hour wears !
A single blast imbrowns the heath,
    The first chill wind his chaplet sears.

XIV.

" October spreads with topaz hue
   Th' autumnal floor, while sad and few
   Are nature's songs, — reflective bent
   Life's faltering steps in slow descent.
   The shadow length'ning on the lea,
   The wan moon's pathway on the sea,
   The deep'ning cadences of day,
   The seething night-lull of the spray, —
   Scarce heard from distant rock-bound shore, —
   All whisper, ' Man, thy life soon o'er ! '

XV.

" Old age slow totters in the glade,
   'Mid cold December's leafless shade ;
   Through joyless nature howls the blast ;
   The mountain torrent surges fast.
   Perchance, in flow of ebbing age,
   The lone and darksome pilgrimage
   Of death begins in life, — when mind
   Hath left a vacancy behind :
   Oblivion mounts her dreamy throne ;
   Her trains of fancies, one by one,
   Recall of childhood hours ; and then
   The agëd smiles, and dreams again.

XVI.

" Now have the three Custodia dread
Spun out, yet pause to cut, the thread
Of weavëd life. The fiat said,
And man is with the mumbling dead,
Where Styx, in dread Gehenna's gloom,
In turgid flow, shall tell his doom!

XVII.

" And this is Syria, whose proud queen
Hath flung her banner 'gainst the sheen
Of purpled Rome! This beauteous land,
The gods on high, with showering hand,
Have ever filled with plenteousness
And fruitful bloom. So Christians say
That Israel was, ere Righteousness
Was lost in Sin ; for in that day
Their valleys smoked with impious flame,
As infants bled for Moloch's name!

XVIII.

" Here did th' Israelitish king —
Earth's wisest — Juda's cohorts bring ;
And Tadmor from the desert rose ;
And here Damascus, where still flows
Her golden stream ! I 've heard, in Rome,

When good Vespasian reigned, did come,
In chains, one Paul, and told that here
A voice from Heaven called him from
His persecuting sin, to bear
Thenceforth the cross of Him who rose
From Calvary, where Kedron flows!
He fell, the Seven Churches fell,
And all who impious would assail
Great Jove, th' Omnipotent of all!

XIX.

" Roma, my country! is *thy* doom
To know decadence, and the tomb
Of this flood's depths? A thousand times
This whirling globe hath rung her chimes
In New-Year peal! as oft her chord
The poisëd sun hath faintly heard
In burning Cancer! — and yet still
Rome's empire is, unbound her will!"

XX.

Now shift the scene to Theudemor!
And mark, that ceaseless-spinning Time
Has passed one half th' Ecliptic floor!
On Suri's genial perfumed clime
.The sacred sun more vertic glows,
To greet her streams, but not the rose!

XXI.

But few the hours to the crash
Upon thy wall, thou lone Tadmor!
For vain the wild Arabians' dash —
Like lightning on the Bætic shore —
Upon the Roman cohorts' mail!
At night, their lances like the gale,
When the crashing cloud lights up the side
Of Athos, and th' Ægean tide.

XXII.

In vain Palmyra's gates wide ope,
Her thousands shower down the slope
To break the siege! In vain the foe
Is thwarted in the mine below!
For angered voice and steelëd clank
Come faintly from the deep-earth dank,
Where gallery has sapped in vain
To turn the stream into the plain;
Or where 't would kindle flame beneath,
And level wall upon the heath.

XXIII.

This night, amid the harshest hum
Of battle-music shrill, shall come
The gath'ring tramp, and moaning wail,
When Tadmor mourns for those shall fall!

XXIV.

O Death! thy sting is not the end
Of mortal life! Man may defend
'Gainst recollections of his joys
To be no more : not this alloys
His parting hour! That horrid grin,
That griping agony, is Sin!

XXV.

Sin frets and clogs the struggling soul!
   To that vast void it may not soar.
Boundless infinitude! the roll
   And noise of all the orbs afar,
Seen from the Caspian, to their full
Accretioned, would be but a toll ;
Nor heard by smallest orb of light
Which shines on Heaven's gorgeous night!
To the just alone decreed the sight, —
By ordinance of the Mighty One, —
In flickering life, to joyous read
The gleaming scroll, "Well hast thou done!"
For him alone, on High decreed,
To see the crystal-studded mounts,
The vales in amber-colored glow,
Where, gushing forth, the living founts
Of precious mercy ceaseless flow!

XXVI.

Land of the lily and the palm !
How oft, in evening hour calm,
The Afric wind has whispered tales
Amid the hush of thy sweet vales,
And told, she lingered on Galilee ;
And there came down from airy height,
At Bethlehem was glad to light,
But sorrowing moaned at Calvary !

XXVII.

Pride of the East, to thee in vain
'T was told, that Christ was born and slain
To rise again ! Yon foam-born queen,
Pure-robed in white and silvery sheen,
Drawn through the azure by her doves,
Fanned by the roseate-smiling loves,
Astarte hight, — for her, Tadmor
And Thammuz, whom she moaned of yore,
And now would glean anemone,
And gladly drink its purple die !
For *these*, by night, thy temples throng,
With chorals sweet, and hymning song !

XXVIII.

Alas ! Bellona's shrieking voice
Through Suri howls with fearful noise ;

And calls her handmaids to her side,
And bids them scatter far and wide
Grim pestilence and famine sear, —
For these to war are ever near!

XXIX.

Quick they obey : and now full soon,
'Mid havoc wild, the fierce triune
On Tadmor's vale and towers fall !
But there divide, — the Roman feels
Full soon disease, which, dreadful, steals
Resistless through his chainëd mail,
Though many a lance had plunged in vain ;
And many a warrior tells this eve
To the babbling camp, 'in glad reprieve,
His day-deeds o'er, who, when again
The morn shall tint each mount and vale,
Shall clutch in death *his own* breast-mail !

XXX.

Sad Theudemor ! thy sacred sun
  Not now to thee distils such dew
Of chill disease. But there is one
  More dreadful woe, — and sparing few.
Want unsupplied ! Mark now the glare
Of the rambling eye, where once the clear

And merry glance of jocund age!
When Rome shall bind more close her siege,
Thou helpless fondling, weep, but heed!
Thou shalt be *fed!* and *death* shall feed!

XXXI.

Why haste to war, ye sons of men?
Alas! the subtle fiend, when,
In hell's profound and dark arcane,
He brewed the brackish slimy juice
For Eve, the compound did infuse
With crimson gall, a venom gum,
With which compared the hemlock sore
Life-giving is! From deep-hell gloom
To Ede he's come! Ede is no more!
Her wandering queen is roaming o'er
The earth exiled, and tells awhiles
Of joy in those once flowery aisles;
And while she speaks, the hand of Cain
Is crimsoned deep, and man slays man!

XXXII.

Why haste to war? The holocaust
Of death has smoked with human gore
With ceaseless flame, from the Borean coast
To South Arabia's myrrhine shore.

Let anger but his conscience sear,
And man would from his adverse tear
The upturned eye, and hush its prayer !

XXXIII.

How different is the olive-grove,
Where smiling Peace may fearless rove ;
Sprung from high heaven and from the earth,
And as to mark such precious birth,
She was enwreathed in blooming flowers,
And in her hand th' averted torch ;
While o'er her bloodless altars watch,
To keep unharmed her tranquil bowers,
Her pearl-crowned sisters, — justice, law.
And over all Astræa keeps —
That heaven-born mother never sleeps —
Her scales well poised. *She* would that o'er
The earth man would but render due
And justice to his fellow-man !
This done, the gales indeed but few
A nation's wrongs could ever fan
From ember to the hideous fires
Of sack and pillage, whose dread pyres
Have burned, and still relentless burn,
In every clime of every zone !

CANTO III.

THE FALL.

CANTO III.

THE FALL.

WHERE, O vain man, has that lost Pleiad
gone,
Which, many ages since, her sisterhood
Of clustering orbs did leave?.   God knows her morn,
Her noon, and eve, and night, as when she stood
The monarch of the stars! She throws a flood
Of light on worlds beyond the mortal ken ;
While He, th' Omniscient, marks her solitude,
And hears her winding spheric-harp's refrain,
When all the other orbs have ceased their choral strain!

I.

Now Erebus, with sable train,
Shadows, darkness, fitful dreams,
His night-march stalks in Syria's glen
All lightless ; for the flinty gleams,
Which nightly there had showered wide
From peak to peak and side to side
Of rocky pass, have flickered out ;

Uncalled the watch, unheard the shout ;
All hushed as tide of Great-sea main.
Sad Theudemor, thou 'lt hear again !

II.

Wearied with watching, and with thought
How next to thwart his Roman foes,
Longinus sleeps ; but not repose
Is there for one whose mind is fraught
With troublous care ! Not thus the swain
Whose day-toil o'er, down-glides the stream
Of sweet oblivion, and whose dream
Will follow its flow with willing brain.

III.

The sable balances of night
Are equal poised 'twixt eve and morn.
Longinus' dream takes distant flight :
" What sound is that by echo borne ? "
He speaks aloud : " Is it the breeze
Which, oft-times checked by clustering trees
Which throng on cypressed Lebanon,
Sweeps wildly o'er the desert lone ?
'T is the Roman pæan ! Rouse, Tadmor !
Thou soon shalt feel a crash and roar
Such as yon walls have ne'er yet known !
List to yon distant measured moan : —

THE PÆAN.

I.

" Fling up the proud eagles, ye sons of Italia !
  Bandrols and banners in glittering sheen !
Our history's pages are gilded yet brighter,
  For Roma has conquered where Roma has seen !
    In the wilds of the North,
    Where the Teuton and Goth
Still dream of the Tibur in midsummer green, —
    Where the Nubian gale
    Fans the dark Nilus' vale, —
Our Roma has conquered where Roma has seen !

2.

" Brave Hellas we levelled e'en to her foundations,
  Her streamlets made dry ere they gushed to the sea ;
And thus shall be darkened this ' Pride of the Morning,'
  And crumbled her colonnades, strong though they
     be !
    We shall give her bright domes
    To the fierce desert-storms, —
Ply sickle and scythe where is Tadmor beneath ;
    Then shout mount to mountain,
    And echo each fountain,
' The gods give Aurelian victory's wreath ! ' "

4

IV.

" Now to the walls ! and from your towers
Mark where the foe would hurl his showers
Of ironed beams and massive rock !
Mark where shall come the storming shock
Of the swinging ram, and the barbed hail,
When shell-bound Plutei assail !

V.

" Drive on your mines ! that hollow earth,
When firm their plumbean tower stands,
With archers crowded in its girth,
Shall yield till scorched and smoking sands,
Long fusing from your flaming brands,
Shall deep engulf them ! List ! more near
The murmur comes ; and, by the glare
Of crackling flames, methinks they bear
In Roman camp the red-flag streaming,
And high spears firm and battle-gleaming !

VI.

" A trumpet sounds ! their leader's voice
Calls to the Milites for choice.
At once are countless hands upthrown ;
At once their voices shout aloud ;
And shields are rung, their flash, upborne,
Enlightens bright yon midnight cloud.

VII.

"Now sound the trumpets' harshest din ;
　'To arms !' the Roman legions cry ;
The eagles willing, they deem to win
　More sure in war the victory.
When standards loathe to leave the ground,
Unheard the shout and triumph-sound.

VIII.

"Their watchword giv'n with furious foam,
Aurelian cries : 'Sons of Rome !
Live not to hear, in days to come,
That ye, who 've conquered the hardy Goth,
And whose proud pæan has sounded north
Till Scythian quailed, — that ye did storm
In vain 'gainst one of woman form !
Fling your banners 'mid the foe !
The gods are ours ; and, ere the glow
Of earliest morn shall tint the east,
Palmyra's ours ! Your toil ceased,
The golden crown shall deck your feast !'

IX.

"And now they summon from our bounds
The guardian gods. Quick now resounds
The hideous crash of angered war !

In vain their shielded tortoise creeps
To mount the high walls' sloping steeps;
The huge rock slips, and with a roar —
Like many whirlwinds in the deeps
Shiver the foam on rocky shore —
Breaks down and bursts their platted shields!
In sad recoil the cohort yields!

X.

"Now let your engines pour their floods
　　Of eager flame upon the foe;
Yon sparkling fire ever bodes
　　Dread ruin in its arrowed flow.
'Now charge, ye steel-clad heroes, down!'
　　See how they stream! Ah! many a groan
Comes up from Roman ranks full soon!
　　Their lines are broken, but not gone.

XI.

"In vain your charge, my noble braves!
But few return, and many graves
Are found amid the din and tramp
And hideous glare of Roman camp.
Aurelian redoubles now
　　His eager legions, for the storm
Is trending, Tadmor, to thy brow;
　　In solid wedge and thick they form!

XII.

"And thou, my queen, art undismayed
  Amid this crash and battle roar!
For thee shall shiver many a blade,
  Ere thou shalt lose thy own Tadmor.
Amid the sound, and 'mid yon sheen,
Is heard thy voice, and marked thy mien.

XIII.

"List! comes the deadliest crash of all!
A hundred engines seek the wall.
Though thousands fall, the mighty beams
Swing to and fro; the iron gleams
Like lightning flash amid the gloom
Of dismal Hades' vale of doom!

XIV.

"Now whirled far back to utmost bound,
They scoop the air with whirlwind sound.
Our walls are crumbling! Fly, thou queen,
While yet the night thy course may screen!
Go thou to Persia! Rome shall know
She has but taken *one* Tadmor.
She's gone! The foe Palmyra gains!
Our *queen* yet lives, and Syria reigns!"

XV.

We leave the harsh discord of war,
And speed the Syrian desert o'er.
See, in yon deep and shaded bower,
The lily, thyme, and myrtle flower,
With citron branch and leaves entwine,
And tendrils drooping from the vine.
Their essence sweet as that which came
From far Sabea, to the child
Who humbly slept in Bethlehem,
While hushed the voicing night-wind wild,
And God to man was reconciled!

XVI.

No sound comes here, save waters' moan
Of fair Euphrates; and the lone
And low chant of the vigil watch,
Who nightly the sacred embers turn,
Till morn doth gild the orient arch
(This night the last that flame shall burn)!

XVII.

Here woman weeps, and weeps alone,
Save but a minstrel; he is one
Of boyhood bloom, and form and face
Of Hylas, when with heavenly grace

He tripped the blue Olympian skies,
And gave the cup to Hercules.

XVIII.

The woman lays a diadem
Upon the ground ; unclasps the gem
Which circled neck and arm.   The seas
Were sounded deep to give her these.
So pure each pearl and diamond rare,
It seemed like morn-dew sprinkled there.

XIX.

Her voice in such sad cadence fell,
It hushed the mellowing warbled trill
Of the Bulbul in her leafy gloom.
And many a floweret lost its bloom ;
For here, 't is said that all night long
The Syrian roses list her song.
Her voice enchimed with river's flow,
She told the child and night her woe !

I.

Is it a dream ? My gilded empire lost,
   Down-trampled to the dust by mighty Rome ?
My firm-foundationed power rudely tost,
   As wild winds lash the shivering ocean foam ?

2.

Fair Suri, I had often longed to bind
　　The nations' crowns upon thy lily brow !
And, proud Italia conquered, naught had lined
　　Thy power's limit, save th' Atlantic flow !

3.

But now, hushed e'en my merry vineyard song
　　In paths once peaceful ; and the trills
Of twilight nature never more shall throng
　　Through Theudemor's acacia-blossomed hills !

4

All pomp and spangled power now have fled !
　　Palmyra, to oblivion doomed, shall be
Unsorrowed and unknown, save by her dead, —
　　As Siddim's lone and ever surgeless sea !

5.

And thou, Longinus, who hast ever been
　　Not *self*, but ministrant to Tadmor's throne !
To regain all that's lost were not to win,
　　If thou, Devotion's fairest type, art gone !

XX.

　　The minstrel deemed by word and smile
　　Her sorrowing anguish to beguile,
　　And 'suage her woe. Then, pausing, sought
　　His lyre, for well he had been taught,

Though young, each cadence and each chord
That skill and nature could afford.
Then rambling o'er its golden strings,
His boyish carol thus he flings :—

I.

See, on fair Persia's glimmered sand,
Sweet Lotis, with her pearly hand,
  Entwines the lily stem.
On th' aloes lute, when Dian's gleam
First silvers o'er Euphrates' stream,
  She chants her evening hymn!

2.

With blithe Aurora's matin-song,
Her nereid-train in clusters throng
  Where blushing corals grow!
Be *thou* so sad, they trip away,
Ere yet the joyous jocund day
  Has kissed Togarmah's snow!

3.

Then bind those temples once again!
O'er Theudemor thou mayst not reign ;
  Deem not the past hath been!
But bid thou gold-winged Hope to tell
Yon wave and wind, in flood and dell,
  Thou shalt be *Syria's* queen!

XXI.

Now morning comes, but clouds of gloom
Enscreen the sun ; his 'customed song
He hears not ; but, as from a tomb,
Wild sorrow urges slow along
The Syrian plain for many a rood ;
And where her pride and plenty stood
In gorgeous glow, now smokes and reeks
With pilëd death ! The searcher seeks
Amid the glaring holocaust
For one faint smile, ere yet be lost
The pulse of life ; while in the air
The flapping bird has fixed his glare.

XXII.

The victory o'er, at trumpets' sound,
The Roman lictors wind around
Their fasces with the laurel leaves ;
And soldier decks his triumph spear,
And decks his horse, who weary heaves,
Though firm his tramp, yet wild his glare !

XXIII.

Already, on his fleetest steed,
A horseman flies with earnest speed
To tell to Rome, " The conflict o'er,

Though hard the siege, we have Tadmor!"
His message bound in brightest green,
He skims across the desert sheen!

XXIV.

The cohorts all assembled now,
'T is known who wins the golden brow;
Who primal scaled the city wall,
Who first from rampart wound the call.

XXV.

How many a soldier glows with pride,
The " Hasta Pura " by his side,
While thousands gaze with envious glance,
As floats the streamer from his lance;
How many a steed is trapped in gold,
And clanking chains of cunning mould,
And broidered lace all covered o'er;
How many a helm the bright horn bore,
'T were vain to tell! for daring deeds
Were done on Syria's sandy meads
Ere Tadmor fell! But speed our tale:
The trumpets sound "Assembly Call"!

XXVI.

On throne of gold, Aurelian
Calls to his side the crownëd train.

For Rome hath ever marked with care
And honor full, the brave in war!
There youth, his primal conflict won;
There veteran, whom storm and sun
Had tinged and furrowed white and deep,
For old his years, and soon his sleep.

XXVII.

For well he knew the battle-blast!
And oft, when first ranks hurried past,
On knee affixed, Triarii
Opposed the storm of charging host;
For well they deemed, if they should fly,
Rome's standard fell, the battle lost!

XXVIII.

The purpled monarch waved about
His ivory sceptre; hushed the shout
Of clanging legions; firm his·look,
And sad, yet proud, as thus he spoke:—

XXIX.

"Captains of Rome! I well may mourn
Your serried ranks, and banners torn!
Six months have rolled since first we cast
Our camp upon this desert waste!
Six moons ye've braved yon orient foe,

And oft have hurled her steel-clad files,
As Euroclydon sweeps the flow
Of waves upon Ægean isles.

XXX.

"For you the triumph and the spoil!
Your deeds were noble, vast your toil!
For our treasured dead, alas! no urn;
For them no cresset-light shall burn.
They fell for Rome, — they need not more
To glide the Stygian billows o'er.
Bring in the captives of Tadmor!"

XXXI.

His voice surceased; but many a tear
Fell free and fast from soldiers there,
Who soothed and sorrowed the parting groan
Of one well loved; his gasping moan
Still rang its cadence o'er and o'er,
And looked "Revenge on Theudemor!"

XXXII.

Where now thy spirit, Orient Queen,
And why dejected in thy mien?
Not thus thy look, when from thy throne
Thou ledd'st thy hosts of legions on

To stormy battle! Canst thou fear
Yon legions' clamor for thy death?
Some deeper woe thy mind must share,
To pale thy cheek and speed thy breath.

XXXIII.

The captives come in gloomy pace
To imperial presence. First of all,
Longinus ; mark a tear downfall
Zenobia's fair but anguished face!
Still proud his look, undimmed his eye,
As when on Tadmor's citadel,
While round him glanced the arrow-hail,
He marked the foe, and how they fell
When swept Palmyra's legions by.

XXXIV.

Unmoved his soul, as Petra's rock,
Which scorns the bleakest-driven shock
Of wild Arabia, whose lone sands,
To utter desolation cursed,
Woo not the gales of happier lands,
But mock the whirlwind's shivering burst.

XXXV.

Now troop the captives, till the plain
Resounds their tread and clanking chain.

Now thrice ten thousand shields are clashed ;
As many spears and lances flashed ;
As many voices shout aloud,
"Give us to death the 'Queen of the East' !
Our fallen, from their silent shroud,
Would call 'Revenge!'   Give us the feast !"

XXXVI.

Like bird of Indian land, which seeks
To burst the charm which binds her eye ;
On fluttering wing, she soars the peaks,
Looks fond at death, yet loath to die ;
So swayed Zenobia's troubled soul,
While on her heart the tempter stole.

XXXVII.

Unshaken as the strong banyan
In sunny Scinde, or Hindostan,
When howls the monsoon's sea-born storm,
So firm Longinus' soul and form !

XXXVIII.

Then spoke the laurelled emperor :
"Thou whilom Queen of Theudemor !
Didst thou, all aidless, urge this war,
So fraught with woe upon our ranks,
That yellow Tibur's teeming banks

Full long shall mourn? Didst thou alone
Contemn the truce by us proposed?
And with more strength thy proud gates closed;
And searched in all the burning zone
For elements to mix that flame,
Which, seething, from thy towers came,
And gnawed corroding through each limb?
In vain the barb was quick withdrawn;
In vain my hero back was borne;
His eye but flashed, and then grew dim.
If thou wast counselled, say by whom?
Thou shalt have life, and *they* thy doom!
Thou wilt not speak? Then, by the Gods!
Though woman, thou shalt die the death!"
Now flash again the Roman swords;
Then silent as, save whispered breath,
When storms are still, Sahara's heath!

XXXIX.

The trembling Queen sees not who comes!
Her eyes downcast, 't is sable forms
Of dark and dread Carnifices!
They reach her ear, though not her gaze.
Zenobia, now strong-brace thy soul,
And thou shalt win the golden goal
Of honored death! A moment more
(For see they fix the fatal block

To meet the axe's stunning shock)
Thy *soul* shall breathe, *earth's* anguish o'er !

XL.

Now o'er her frame a tremor cold
Quick chilled the tear which else had rolled.
Her quivering hand slow moves, 't is raised,
It rests.   Longinus, — it is he !
As the firm martyr, when high blazed
At first the pyre, drooped his knee,
Then, springing up, the brand he seized,
And smiled to immortality !

XLI.

So did Longinus know one pang,
His pure heart bitter venom feel ;
Not serpent's thirsting eager fang
So soon his life-pulse could make still !
"'T is done !"   He speaks : "One moment more,
I shall but rest with thee, Tadmor ;
Full soon, amid destroying showers,
Shall crash thy temple and thy towers !

XLII.

" Thou, Imperator ! mayst not claim
That *thou* hast silenced Tadmor's name !
Palmyra hath herself destroyed ;

5

O, sad her fall, and gloom her void!
And thou, unhappy Queen, live on!
Amid Rome's joy, thy jewelled crown
Will be as bright as when it shone
O'er thine own Suri! Thou canst tell,
In days to come, of how they fell
Who loved this land, and loved it well!

XLIII.

"For you, my friends in doom! the tide
And time are apt that we unmoor
Our vessels from life's harbor-side,
And sail the boundless blue-deep o'er
With hopeful helm! Our precious freight,
The triune soul, shall joyous gain
Eternal bliss, nor long shall wait
In doubtful wind or adverse main!"

XLIV.

Longinus ceased; and then, once more,
He turned to th' Orient and Tadmor!
"Bring here the block!" The shimmering blade
At once upsprings! Longinus dead!

XLV.

Go thou to Syria, where the gale
Still winds along her blasted vale;

And in the desert thou shalt find
An Arab lone ; he strives to bind
Some fallen frieze with moistened clay.
He has toiled full long, for the crimson day
To the West glides down ; the sun is wan
When ling'ring on sad Suristan !
'T is eve ! the toiler's work is o'er ;
Lone Arab, tell ! Was *this* Tadmor ?

Cambridge : Printed by Welch, Bigelow, & Co.

www.ingramcontent.com/pod-product-compliance
Lightning Source LLC
Chambersburg PA
CBHW022021080426
42733CB00007B/679